TICKNER'S
HORSES

LAUGHS FROM HORSE *and* HOUND

· THE SPORTSMAN'S PRESS ·
LONDON

Published by The Sportsman's Press in 1986

Reprinted 1987 © Horse and Hound 1986

British Library Cataloguing in Publication
Data

Tickner, John
  Tickner's horses: laughs from Horse and
  Hound.
  1. Horsemanship–Caricatures and
  cartoons
  2. English wit and humour, Pictorial
  I. Title II. Horse and Hound
  741.5'942   NC1479

  ISBN 0-948253-09-6

Printed and bound in Great Britain at
The Bath Press, Avon

FOREWORD BY MICHAEL CLAYTON

"When are you going to produce Tickner's *Horse and Hound* cartoons in a book?".

The question has been constantly asked by many of our readers since John Tickner's cartoons appeared every week in our magazine. I am delighted that The Sportsman's Press has now made this possible, and I am sure there will be an enthusiastic response from John's many admirers throughout the world of *Horse and Hound*.

He delights and teases all who aspire to ride or drive horses and ponies, and I think he is especially gifted in deftly illuminating the foibles of the hunting field.

In this, he continues with distinction a great tradition of British sporting cartoons. John's high standard of draughtsmanship, his deep knowledge of horses and country ways, and acute powers of observation, are all formidable weapons in his armoury as a cartoonist.

Above all, of course, he unfailingly captures the attention of *Horse and Hound* readers by the expression of his own brand of humour, which is warm and friendly, even when it is putting an unerring finger on mankind's follies in endeavouring to control horse or hound.

Putting Tickner's *Horse and Hound* cartoons between hard covers is long overdue, and I am sure this book will have a valued place in the homes of the many thousands whose week is incomplete without his unique contribution to the "bible of the horse world".

Michael Clayton
Editor of *Horse and Hound*

SHOW JUMPING AND SHOWING

"I'm sure she's come straight from the leading-rein class."

"We'll be going on in a minute, he's just cooling off."

"Our new horse will do anything to avoid knocking jumps down."

"Now if they had a class for the awkward horse of the year."

"Show jumping gets rather monotonous, doesn't it?"

"She's awfully keen, doesn't let a fall stop her."

"I told her it would be bad form to wear wellies!"

"You got the name wrong again!"

"I don't think he's keen on going to shows."

"I don't understand people who spend the day
on a crowded beach."

"I dislike this foreign dressage jargon; give me a village gymkhana where everyone wears jodhpurs and the lingo is pukka English."

"They always walk like that; they're dressage judges."

"That's cheating, boy!"

"Thank goodness we don't get any violence at these shows!"

"She's held the cup for the last two years."

"Remember what you said about the grey last year?"

"You wouldn't think their ancestors were wild,
untamed creatures."

"We had a good cup-hunting season, I see!"

EVENTING AND TEAM CROSS-COUNTRY

"Loose dogs can be an embarrassment!"

"The eventing season will soon be over and then we can get down to serious sport."

"I don't really understand eventing – some of it goes over my head."

"You get a much better splash at three-day events than at these hunter trials."

"You're just playing to the gallery!"

"Keep together, team!"

"The great thing about team events is the togetherness."

J. TICKNER

RACING AND POINT-TO-POINT

"The owner breeds gundogs."

"One indication of the connection between hunting and point-to-point racing is the sporting jargon."

"It is much better on television."

J. TICKNER

"He's awfully good on water skis."

"Ladies' race."

"My niece is the pretty blonde one."

J. TICKNER

DRIVING

"She must have heard you call her Boadicea
the first time round."

"I am sure it's not as heavy as it was when we started!"

J. TICKNER

"She reserves the horse for the summer shows."

"I told you we should have turned left!"

J. TICKNER

"Those driving people tackle some extraordinary obstacles."

LONG DISTANCE RIDING

"I have not lost the way and those are not vultures!"

"Nobody shot him! He says he gets tired on these long distance rides."

"I think he is left over from a previous long distance ride."

HUNTING AND HOUNDS

"Lawn meet."

J. TICKNER

"I see there are some new loose horses out this season."

"No dear – they're the wrong sort of cubs!"

"I love early cubhunting – isn't it grand to be up when most folk are in bed!"

"Cubhunting is the ideal opportunity to let children see what it's all about."

"That's not the field. They're the Joint Masters."

"The Secretary is liable to drop on one unexpectedly."

"That could be the record for a horseless high jump."

"Will he jump the water?"

"My New Year resolution is to make sure that all gates are shut."

"We have a very strong supporters' club."

J. TICKNER

"Don't let me catch you galloping madly about!"

"He's been a menace since he saw the
Spanish Riding School display!"

"Nobody told him the horse is an eventer – loves quarries."

"Because he won a cup he thinks he's dog's gift to bitches."

J. TICKNER

"And if we need your help we'll let you know."

"So I jumped on the fox, like this!"

"Here come the winter seasonal workers again!"

"That reminds me – I haven't ordered a bird for Christmas!"

"Tomorrow we'll take them over that line of nasty drop fences."

"It must be inflation – I only got a stale sausage roll this time."